Korean Letters

Korean Letters
Poems

David Cameron

POCKET POEMS

Also by David Cameron

Poetry

The Bright Tethers: Poems 1988–2016

Fiction

Rousseau Moon

The Ghost of Alice Fields

Prendergast's Fall

Criticism

Samuel Beckett: The Middle and Later Years

davidcameronpoet.com

For my mother, Mary,
& in memory of my father, George

Acknowledgements
Aiblins: New Scottish Political Poetry (Luath Press), A Kist of Thistles: An Anthology of Radical Poetry from Scotland (Culture Matters), Glasgow Review of Books, Horse Power (Federation of Writers, Scotland), Poetry Salzburg, Silk and Smoke, The Blue Nib, The Dark Horse, The Island Review, The Moth, The Ramingo's Porch

Published in 2020 by Rune Press Ltd., London, England

www.runepress.com

Printed and bound in Great Britain by
TJ Books Ltd., Padstow, Cornwall

Typeset by Stephen Cameron, Glasgow, Scotland

ISBN: 978-0-9574669-8-2

Contents

AUTHOR'S NOTE

Almost all of the poems in this book were written in the four years since the publication of *The Bright Tethers: Poems 1988 to 2016*. Like the poems in that pocket-sized red book, the poems in this pocket-sized blue book fit the definition I gave there of my poetry as 'a sudden revelation, but of something I realised I had always known'.

Letting go, finally, of so many poems at once did have a liberating effect. I became more prolific than before, and I was already (since moving to Ireland and starting a family) the most prolific I had ever been. And I wrote – at over two hundred lines – the only long poem to be found in my work. But even this wasn't a studied affair. For a number of years now I have almost never written, or typed, a poem; mainly because lines come to me when I'm without notebook, pen or computer – such as on the drive in to Belfast in the mornings. Now this reliance on memory has become an article of faith, or at least a superstition. If I forget some lines – well, that just means they weren't memorable.

An obvious objection is: how could this principle have applied in the case of the book's title poem, which consists entirely of words written in letters home by my father when he was on National Service in Korea? I had been typing up for my brothers the deteriorated fragments of letters (they were a lifeline to the memory of the man we had all four of us lost at a young age) when some phrases and sentences started to repeat in my head. I had thought these words would be a starting-point for a new poem of my own, but I ended up acting as vehicle not ventriloquist. The origins of this apparently contrived poem were just as involuntary as those of the other poems here.

The book ends with a cycle of poems that were recently set to music by the Toronto-based composer, David Jaeger. This is the third cycle we have collaborated on to date, and there have also been individual pieces: some compositions are for unaccompanied voice, some for piano and voice (soprano, mostly), some for cello and others for piano and recitation (by me). Several of the pieces have been performed in Toronto and Belfast, and (since lockdown) in various online settings. I would like to put on record my gratitude to David for stirring, in a new way, my passion for music and the word.

David Cameron

KOREAN LETTERS

1
Nettie, your fears of the Formosa Straits
Were unfounded,
As we sailed on the opposite side.
I have sent you a postcard of Singapore.

2
I'm in the transit camp at Kure.
I don't know how long I'll be here.
So until you receive a definite address,
There is no point in writing.

3
One hears of the atrocities,
Some isolated cases
Of British soldiers foully murdered.
I suppose some of these tales are true.

4
The school children all wear long trousers,
Buttoned-to-the-neck jackets, and peaked caps.
The women, except for the prostitutes,
Wear long skirts with a high waistline.

5
Language is a barrier but I have tried
To carry on a conversation
With pidgin English and signs –
Mostly with signs.

6
The Glasgow Fair will be in full swing by now.
Just think, if I was at home,
I would probably be away myself.

Now I'm in Korea, 11,000 miles from home.

7
I was deeply grieved to hear
Of the sudden death of Mrs Finlayson.
There must be some reason for birth and death
Which conforms to a pattern in the universe.

8
Glad you are both keeping well.
No need to worry about me, Ma.
I'll come home safe and sound.
I've still got the key to let myself in.

Assembled verbatim from fragments of letters written by the poet's father, George Cameron, while on National Service in Korea.

NO MORE

I speak as over a grave still
Hoping you will come out to play,
And this is not possible.
There are no more words to say.

There are no more words to say.
In the picture I have of you,
You are laughing and dressed brightly,
The sky behind you is blue.

MARINE LIFE

Time to take up my staff, to go
Into homelier regions, where the sun shines
On the miserable householder,
Where breadvans scout the towns.
Here children, eyes like marble,
Gathered in rings or playing fivestones,
Point the way to go. To be like them
You must first enter the Kingdom of Heaven:
Impossible journey, given up
As soon as I began it. On the table
Beside me I have some shells, stones,
And picked flowers in a broken cup.
It is everything I know
Of joy, limitation. Like the sea,
The narrow sea returning to the shore,
Having the power to contain me.

AND NOW

I adored you. Back in the day,
I used to walk two miles
To the East Newington cafe
You student-waitressed in.
You would bring me stale buns, fresh smiles
At the end of your shift,
And I would tell you my no-news.
You miss that. My adoring you.

And now? Now, like you, I adore
Our children, crave their smiles,
Clap as one rises from the floor,
Clap as the other dances,
All the time walking the two miles
Near the end of your shift
To bring you more of my no-news.
You miss that. My adoring you.

A LETTER

We're cabin'd, cribb'd, confin'd, as the man said,
But that's all right. Love's febrile, it survives
Not-quite-contempt-bred glances over cornflakes.
Our cabin fever only goes to show
Our love, which would lie greenly in long grass.
Look back through my letters: didn't I write
That it so happens you contain the sky?
Here, where all feel cramped, I look down at clouds
That are a lover's dream. Tempting miracle,
The wing says not to walk outside. It's odd
To have this demon for a pilot always
And still feel safe, and speak of love as lasting,
In cabins where the pressure seldom drops.

MOOD MUSIC

The music of a murderous mood
Which doesn't know that it is murderous
Until it sees loved eyes awash with tears,
This mood music could

Be melancholy, on a minor chord
Lamenting 'sunburned hands I used to hold',
Or some insulting waltz from *Classic Gold*
Leading you, without a word,

To the steepening cliff edge. Next,
You'll hear it with a less-constricted heart
In the kitchen, comfortably as 'art',
The damage it accompanied unfixed.

FOUR ELEGIES

IRON MAN

for Sean Fallon, assistant manager to Jock Stein at Celtic

My mum to my dying aunt:
'Mind the time Sean Fallon danced us both.'
The Iron Man lies in my home town now
As I sit here, a short drive from his:
Sligo, that 'sorrowing drunk' of a town,
The poet said. Not like this best of sons –
An uncoverer of gems in his field;
Part of a double act, the perfect foil;
A dancer in the earth of Philipshill.

REELING
for Dermot Healy

I dreamt there was a rustling outside,
Opened the door and saw a dead blackbird
Hover, an inch in the air, and then twitch.
How could a dead bird do that? It was a wire
Under a wing, working it, a wire
Which I unhooked
And held one-fingered, like a fishing-line,
And followed to its source. The source was you
High on a hill, not rooting among stones
At your Atlantic-battered, bulwarked home.
'You see,' you said, 'I outsmarted you all.'
Not I you, but you had reeled me in.

It was the next day, Dermot, that I heard.

HAND SHADOWS

for the 'young British poet', Robert Nye

My friend, you were first introduced to me as young,
Though you were bearded already, eyes heavy-lidded,
As you spoke of darker ends. Being darkly begun,
I heard the fright in your words – words that sounded whispered
Not to wake your son. Those floating, candlelight-fringed
Wall animals – 'personal beasts' – spoke to me, grandson
Of a woman made by austerity (just once)
Unguardedly happy. That night's serious fun
Linked buoyancy and fear with words packed tight in me.
The surge of energy a power cut produced
Was like the force in Thomas's green fuse, its flower
A truth made beautiful by being pent up then loosed.

THIS LIFE
for Jack Ross

Relaxed, manly, with beard and eyes
Not unlike *Serpico* Pacino's,
You had the warm authority
That kindly teachers have. It goes

Like this: I'm back, not in your class –
I never was – but on your sofa
(I wouldn't have you be without
Netta, young Jack or Nicola);

We're playing at being what we are,
Happy families, although we know
That every mug gets chipped in time,
No lawn's without its passing shadow

Which doesn't always pass. Dear Jack,
I've put the LP in its sleeve;
You tell me, 'Take it home – to keep,'
And we get slowly up to leave.

Now all that's gone, and I can be
Nimble and quick, Jack, if I choose,
Except I feel an urge to savour
This life that isn't ours to lose.

SONG: DELIVERED

I'm the old man with a cup
Makes you look through your pockets.
I'm armed with a coathanger
And a fistful of dockets.
I paid off my creditors
The only way I know how.
Whistle Streets of London,
I milk the cream from the cow.

I don't want to be delivered.
I don't want to be delivered.
Bring me back to the depot.
Bring me back to the devil.

Ever seen a camel bleeding
When it's been walked too much?
Ever heard a nail weeping,
A wave ask for a crutch?
I can say I've done stuff
That Genghis Khan can't.
Even the Hare Krishnas
Creep away when I chant.

I don't want to be delivered.
I don't want to be delivered.
Bring me back to the depot.
Bring me back to the devil.

You eat a fudge sundae,
Drink Egyptian spice tea,
A black speck on your eyeball
– Well, that black speck is me.
Somebody say something
Or I'll curl up your toes.
I know places on the river
Where nobody goes.

I don't want to be delivered.
I don't want to be delivered.
Bring me back to the depot.
Bring me back to the devil.

THE SINGLE LINE

He veered off into verges,
As if the passing cars were girls at school
(Under whose scrutiny he blushed),
Hoping against hope
That in *this* field the miracle would come.
And something did come;
Despite the wind that he whipped up,
It came singly, not whole:
The blood-red leaf and the planetary soul.

Oh son (I tell myself),
It is not good for strangers in their cars
To spot the young fall into fields
Except as lovers do.
Your barren time will pass, and be redeemed
Much like the second thief;
So let me twice give back to you
The single line I stole:
The blood-red leaf and the planetary soul.

DISPLACED

Not till I saw their well, no longer there,
Did I appreciate that poverty
Beats rootedness to earth, displacing people
Who must have known a lonely kind of joy
Before herding together on train, steamship.

FROM THE CAR

'Follow it home,' my daughter said,
Seeing a yellow moon from the car.
Sweet girl, I don't need told. It's in my nature
To be moon-led.

DEAR MRS NING-NING

I think of you and how you stare, bed-ridden,
At the absence around your bed
(Or do you populate it now with ghosts
Of son and husband, such
As played at cards on holiday,
Philosophised on sofas, drinking
Into the wee small hours, enjoyably?)
I only came to say
Thank you for teaching me to tie
My laces in a double knot,
A lesson that has served me well.
You won't recall your patience then,
Kerbside in sunny Blackpool,
When my dazed face looked up at yours
Then down again. Your nimble fingers
Slid a loop through the smallest space,
Retreating till mine did the same.

They did, I did, all right, considering
You weren't quite my mother, Mrs Ning-Ning.

YEATS'S EPITAPH

Yeats drafted four lines for his epitaph.
The first, 'Draw rein, draw breath', although as good,
Would never join the rest to make a jingle.
It looms above them like a horseman's hood.

BACK TO BROOD

Words that mean, words that sing:
Eliot wrote, 'Time present and time past
Are both perhaps present in time future,' and Yeats
'Of what is past, or passing, or to come';
Then there's the dismissive line of my mum,
Like an undetailed litany of her pet hates,
Which takes me back to brood on what will last –
'This, that and the next thing.'

EK HAIKU

'East Kilbride, town of tomorrow'

1
'Glasgow overspill',
like some human detritus.
By that they mean us.

2
Vulgar to live in
streets named by committee whim,
not like ours: 'Blackbraes'.

3
Skinned knees from red ash.
No cry-babies in my team,
the Wingate Midgets.

4
The Calderwood shops
our harvest-metropolis.
Wait for the Green Man.

5
There, for the stomach,
butcher, baker; for the head,
library, dentist.

6
Reading Kerouac,
'There is next to no culture
here at all.' Next to?

7
Polo Mint City:
and king of the roundabouts,
the killer Whirlies.

8
Meet me at the pipe
where we'll watch the waste water
slip into the burn.

9
New town, new graveyard.
None aspired to be dead.
Drink from the chained cup.

10
Lawrentian moon,
now that I'm reading Lawrence,
whitening the braes.

THE NEWS

We heard the news the boy had died
And, being boys ourselves, we laughed
Till, seeing how our mother cried,
We kidded on that we were daft.
Before her tears, a primal scream
And urge to know: had that poor woman
Not suffered enough? Like a dream
Of someone only partly human,
News of the boy's death left him out.
Whenever, in our new-town lives,
Death happened at a roundabout,
The brunt seemed borne by mothers, wives,
While boys like us and dads like ours
Were left to bring, or be brought, flowers.

HAD YOU LIVED

Death's milestones never touched me much:
I could endure being the age you were
As I could endure being longer-lived.
No, what got to me
Was realising – had you lived,
You'd now be old enough to die.
Though no tears fell, my heart sank.
How could the living compete
With the ferocious faithfulness
Of the dead? This, I'd thought, sustained me;
Instead,
It was the thought of you at thirty-eight,
Cycle clips on, dark hair slicked back:
Our dad, impervious to death.

INHERITANCE

Some things it's necessary to pass on:
Respect for the sacred, a love of reading;
But saying 'long press', 'put the immersion on'?
The Tooth Fairy's on a par with Christ bleeding
If you're indiscriminate. Once, my son
Came home downcast, looked at me searchingly
And asked: was Santa real? It seemed, just then,
Wrong to lie. 'Do you *really* think that we
Are able to afford all *that*?' (We weren't.)
So, yes, it takes a mix of things to thrive –
Whatever we inherit, what's inherent,
And what of that's passed on. I could survive
To hear my son, glued to a screen and faithless,
Tell his son, 'Have a look in the long press.'

BOY AND MAN

Spending time alone with a woman, at night,
When she's distracted by grief or other things,
A boy has trouble telling left from right.

He won't know – though he'll seek – an intenser room.
And one day, when another says she's hopeful,
Me too, he'll joke, *despite my cloak of gloom.*

EVERYTHING

Slip of the tongue:
'Do you want help with everything?'
– Said casually to one I'd more than helped
And who, roles reversed, might have hung

Me out to dry.
Going from *any* to *every*thing
Is just another slip that can't be helped,
Right? There is no point asking 'Why?'

Except
If I could take back everything
And live again. The one I should have helped
I harmed instead. That can't be side-stepped.

THE EXHIBITION

It was as if you'd spread a sepia wash
Over the work, making it, frankly, dull.
To trick the eye? Whose? Into seeing what?
Care revealed
Not antique paintings needing restoration
But something – well, 'contemporary'? No,
Alive. 'Her new vein: ironic-modern,'
A catalogue might say. You're never that.

Where was our daughter?
Since you were busy with your work again –
As, gratingly, I'd urged – you'd left
Me to mind her. Now she was gone!
Yet you were placid;
She'll come to no harm, your look said. Relief,
To see her there, in a far corner of the square,
Where all your celebrated paintings were

– Celebrated, but a curator hovered,
Muttered critically.
I knew this dead Wagnerian from home,
Challenged him: 'That's my *wife*.'
And your response if I'd put up my paws?

'Come off it. He is the critic in you.
So what if I disguise my true intention?
You with your antique rhymes:
What's metre but a kind of patina?
You think our work won't age? That our love won't?'

None of this was said. I sloped off,
Startled to see your sketchbooks on display,
With a message to me, by name: 'Don't do it'
Spelled out in pennies (no, look closer, cents).

We're alive, not ageless. Can we agree
Not to use washes – sepia or white? I'll try
To have more sense.

HEART

I thought it ornament not animal,
But no, I must rely on its restraint –
The thing I can rely on least of all –
Should love now turn away from its own taint.

CRIME AND PUNISHMENT

It is the saddest thing I've read:
How the crazed, ruble-less step-mother
Goads Sonya into prostitution –
'What's there to protect? Some treasure!'

Ingenuous holy sinner
Or implausible angel-whore
With a 'yellow ticket' ID,
Issue of the Russian Empire.

No need to suspend disbelief.
When she picks up the big green shawl,
Covers her head with it, lies down,
I believe that. That's when tears fall.

THE TANGENTS

Sylvia, my daddy died too
And so loomed large, not Führer-like,
More Mitchum with a dash of Peck.
You gave me a map to my fear.
'The villagers never liked you' –
Words that seemed sudden, almost hidden,
Signposted, on your one-way street,
The tangents that grief lures us down
(Not many now say, 'How dare she
Speak ill of her father like that?').
If anyone can bring me back
To the trail I thought had gone cold
Of fearful capes, killed mockingbirds
And, near the knuckles, LOVE and HATE
To arrive at my daddy driving
A dog sled over Arctic ice,
Sylvia, Sylvia, it's you.

BUDDY HOLLY

The nerdy look, the voice that is God's gift
To parody, being pitched now high, now low,
With little hiccups and an Elvis warble:
He's like the uncle you don't want to know

Who starts to interest then fascinate.
Not just the story that his widowed bride
Recounts of how his quick death in a cornfield
So shocked her that their unborn baby died;

Untragic detail like the name the Crickets
Metamorphosing 'Quarrymen' to 'Beatles';
And, for you, the tremulous affectation
Deserting him in just two syllables:

Mah Peh-ggy Sue. You feel them tug, in turn:
The voice that strains, the voice in slick control;
One that belongs to accident and death,
One to the early days of rock and roll.

MY WORD FOR YOU

for Catriona Cameron

When Frankie Miller sang about being lonesome
And told his girl he'd call her on the phone some
But he didn't have a dime

I wondered what a phonesome was, and why
Glaswegian Frankie wouldn't spend a penny
And found it hard to mime.

My boyish puzzlement could not mistake
The brilliance of the singer or his heartache
When he sang 'Darlin'. And darling

Has been my word for you, sweet niece, your whole life.
In my head, when you turn to us, a wife,
'Darling,' I'll sing.

MATINEE MOVIE TIME

THE RAZOR'S EDGE

Memorably, for I remember,
Tyrone Power ('Larry') quotes John Keats
After Anne Baxter ('Sophie') dies.
She was a friend who'd had, and lost,
'A sort of lovely purity'.

Reproach is easy; the compassion
Larry shows Sophie isn't that.

The day is gone, and all its sweets are gone!

DON'T LOOK NOW

Blindness equals prescience. Heather
Can 'see' the danger Baxter's in,
Pursuing through Venetian streets
A seeming girl in a red mac.
He knows she isn't his drowned daughter,
But maybe this time he can save her.

The blindness dovetails with my sorrow
But all are deaf to my prescient cry:
Let him not go!

VERTIGO

When Scottie tackles Judy in the bell-tower
Of the Spanish mission, telling her twice
'You were a very apt pupil,' the aptness
Of *apt* itself is more than doubtful. Yet
Passionate inexactitude is right:
He'd courted the accomplice of a murderer.

THE GODFATHER

When Michael Corleone walked with Kay
Through snowy New York streets at Christmas-time
Hours before life changed unalterably,
Setting the young war hero on the path
To infamy as a dead-eyed mafia don,
It was Christmas! In New York! In the snow!
The future must have seemed within his grasp
As surely as those gifts from Best & Co.

What a dull movie that life would have made.
Instead, Fate dealt the Devil from the Tarot,
So robbing him of spontaneity
(A devil can't be careless) he became
A Method actor studying his own life.
On screen, it's not *The Bells of St Mary's* now:
He can't be saved, though arm-in-arm with Kay
He walks through streets whose snow's been washed away.

WHERE DOGS GO

When the family dog is put down and its owners
Say how it's happy on a farm, the tears
Kids shed are for themselves: the dog is living
The life of dog-Riley. So guilt joins loss
While grown-ups are let off the hook, unless
One, perspicacious, fathoms everything.

My own by-miracle-granted, much-asked-for pet
Was fretted over till my mum could fret
No more. What became of that border collie?
I like to think the story of the farm
True, that only chased rabbits came to harm.
'I like to think' – words kept for every folly.

ELEPHANT

We planned it to a T:
Our guests would go by boat
From a berth near the church
To the medieval *Schreierstoren*
That was no Weeping Tower for us.
Then, days before the wedding,
On a reconnaissance mission,
We saw, on the tower's balcony,
A plastic, full size elephant.

Installed for some arty reason,
Not soon to be taken down,
It made us weep inside,
But nothing could be done;
We just got on with things.
And then the gaudy elephant
Proved a hit with our guests:
The old patted its flanks,
The young slid down its trunk.

Love, let's rein in the metaphor.
Some things just can't be planned for.

PANIC

Panic's no picnic:
The stairwell in the dark,
The felt-for banister, no breath of air.
To grieving eyes, a rain-wet garden
Harbours a kind of consolation;
Panicked eyes find none.
No peace can be had with the spiteful,
Mad remnant of unnerving anger.
Behind the curtains, with your head so sick,
The light of day is fizzing at the sill,
Soon to elongate and harden
Before the unreflective dogs will bark.

Imagined hell. Though not beyond imagining
When your young blood was racing.
Your defence, then, the ever-changing clouds
(But even they, at times, seemed panicking),
That doomed romantic flight in song.
What was the most feared thing –
Which always happens, as Pavese said?
Death? No, the wound being opened for inspection.
You'll find the banister again,
Not shake the dread
That all such episodes
Are merely preludes.

YOU USED TO SING

You used to sing *Hey Jude* to me.
You stayed that age while I grew older.
You used to catch me, swing me up.
I was the movement on your shoulder.

You kept a pen in your shirt pocket –
I'm guessing that I played with it,
Then reached around to your sleeve garter.
You left me guessing quite a bit.

I still had music on the telly.
Leaning my elbow on Mum's knee,
I'd feel again what happened to you
And whatever happened to me.

FRIEZE

The hippy priestess with raised arms intoned:
'In the place of the Father comes the Son.'
The gigolo stretched out like her dead husband,
The helpful pimp – the balding, fumbling one –
Left Oedipus, desireless, in no doubt
That it was up to him to sort her out.

THE SEVENTIES

You never thought your flares and cheesecloth
Would look as dated as they do,
The album covers you pored over
Be outsized junk of card and glue.

What did you think? Only your old dear's
Music and clothes were sure to fade?
Or time would stop to let you off?
It's not in this or that decade

But *now* that life is fresh. So, talk
About the early Doctors Who
And Baader-Meinhof, Chopper bikes,
And what the Eighties did to you.

ALONE WITH YOU

I was the youngest, young enough
To be left behind to do stuff
Like holiday alone with you.
I soaked the winkles in the pail
And teased each winkle from its shell:
I didn't know what else to do.

We walked along the promenade.
You barely hid that you were sad
Or plain bored by my talk of school.
Eyes down, we covered numbers up,
Ate salted chips from the chip shop,
And through it all, I felt – a fool.

How did you feel? You never did
Explain, and I was just a kid
With a pail to put water in.
And the winkles – what did they do
But keep me separate from you;
And was it this preserved us then?

REVOLUTION'S A-SIDE

I am the fruit of Glasgow overspill
Whose paths were still being paved under their feet.
They upped sticks for a stake in urban-idyll
Dreams forged in new technology's white heat.

Then my dad, knocked down on his way to work
At Christmas-time, was dead by New Year's Day.
Our reticence conspired with wintry murk,
Gifting despair a heartless victory.

That set the twin-tub going for a year
Or two, the windows hanging from their rope:
The deeper the clean, the deeper the fear.
Except at night, no tears; some hoped-for hope.

On the label's halved apple, REVOLUTION:
The B-side of the song Dad sang to me;
Now was a time for B-sides, substitution
Of music for grief, played mechanically

Like the piped music heard on Rothesay pier
When a big boat came in. Drunks sang the chorus.
That was our holiday, year after year,
The hamper with our things in sent before us;

I loved the Queen Mary, demure as Mum,
The hard-working Waverley, but I can't
Pinpoint the day I heard new engines thrum:
MV Glen Sannox with the lion rampant.

The room that was my dad's dark room developed
Into a great-aunt's final resting-place;
Then when my gran was knocked down as she shopped,
Its dressing table mirror showed *her* face.

Now there were iced gems for a rain-wet boy
Ushered out of his clothes: welcome affection
That differed from the joy of a new toy,
Dispensed by an octogenarian

Who soon grew tired of me, and my shrill needs.
'Get out the kitchen, you dirty dog, you,'
She'd snap, her hands when free of rosary beads
Busy with tapioca, Irish stew.

There were women with patient skill in school,
Also my blonde queen. I would move her here
Or here, magnetised, obeying my rule.
The moves were hers in real life, that was clear.

And she did move, her hand upon my hand
In the dark of the television room.
On and off like the set, we took a stand
For love that flew by all the nets of home.

'Come down my bit tonight' – an invitation
To hang about the swings, watch 'characters'
(An epileptic girl, loblolly men),
The zones of love confined still to our fingers.

My amorousness, treated as a joke,
Was just a shoogly peg for me to hang from.
The hangmen were my brothers. No one spoke
Of why I'd need *amour*, how much, from whom.

Siblings aren't just rivals. I'll not forget
The time he joined me, held a tiny cup
From my Alice in Wonderland tea-set,
Won as prize; me in a foyer, looking up

To see my own face beaming back at me,
From the time I sat for him; my chilblains
Against a gas fire grille after a day
Spent leafleting, the first of his campaigns.

Three brothers in those 'he' and 'his' and 'him'.
We shivered over records in mid-winter
As *Greasy slicked-down, groovy leather trim*
Changed to *No future, no future, no future...*

Not in the same boat, but on the same waters,
We rocked our bodies in the room above
A woman fated not to have the daughters
She wanted, who would stay and show her love.

By concentrating hard on something sunlit,
I maybe couldn't fly, but I could float
An inch or two above the swirling carpet:
Easy to do when your mum's grown remote.

Beneath the hood the child was turning man,
And after years of just such concentration
Words came, and that's how poetry began;
It was the A-side to that REVOLUTION

– A better substitute for my dad's singing
Than any I have known. Goodbye, Waverley,
Goodbye, Queen Mary, it's another bringing
Me to a port that's stonier and grey.

No insult can be levelled at a Scotsman
That can't be countered with, 'Aye, that's right, pal,
And don't forget it.' I crawled, walked and ran.
I am the fruit of Glasgow overspill.

SKETCH

The skull of my sketch makes Miss flinch,
Or else it's the tool they used to trepan.
She'll put her hand to her throat in a minute.
Less than.

We don't believe in demons any more.
Spend less time on the ancients, she says.
Something more up-to-date:
The NHS.

I feel my skull.
That's where the bore-hole would be.
That's the place where my demons would
Leave me.

Aim for the railing.

TOMBOY

She being the tomboy of the team,
And so an actual girl, can't go
Out of school bounds to play with us.

The boys can go, not the tomboy.
She's as good as any of us,
We say. It's what the Head says goes.

If she can't, none of us will go.
Two, three peel off, and we agree:
It's good for her to play with girls.

I see her eyes – a girl's, a tomboy's –
As the penny drops. Always the eyes.

SCIENCE WITH MY MOTHER

I'd seen it all before:
The gas taps, Periodic Table;
The elementary school book
With seemingly divergent
But actually parallel lines
And two-faced Rubin's vase.
I walked those corridors in summer
With my technician mother;
'A stink of chemicals' is right;
That's science for you.

So why did the vase seem mystical,
The Periodic Table holy scripture,
The curved taps veiled acolytes,
The lines a stretched chequerboard
On which a naked model lay
Dark-haired with bold neck veins
To help explain anatomy?
I walked those corridors in summer
With my technician mother.
That was science for me.

RAFFLES

The suave, pearls-fingering, unrepentant thief,
Raffles, in the afternoon. A cad, sir!
High-born bosomy ladies turned to gooseflesh,
Fleeced by this kleptomaniac-cricketer.

The Yorkshire Television adaptation
Had it all: stagy acting, creaking sets,
Forgettable, mournfully jaunty theme tune,
And amateurish, partly hand-drawn credits.

Raffles himself, through sloppy post-lunch languors,
Gave licence to do wrong. Did I do wrong?
Being left alone made vice compulsory;
Vicious, if you were left alone too long.

'You must not make a criminal the hero,'
Whined Conan Doyle, who hadn't lived to see
A mafioso played by Al Pacino
Orchestrate death with brooding sympathy.

This thief played by a man called Valentine
Made crime pay handsomely. Is life like that?
Would any of those sumptuous ladies fawn
Over the junkie fuck who robbed my flat?

A PLEA

What's wrong with me? I pleaded.
It was a plea, not a question.
I counted on you saying, *Nothing.*

You always know what's needed.
And when I ask, *What's one plus one?*
I'm counting on you saying, *Something.*

DIFFERENTLY

My wife at 29, in a blue jumper,
Holding our first-born, smiling plaintively,
Fills me with deep desire: first, for her;
Next, for a time I would have back again
Only if I could live it differently
And better (less the temper, money worries,
And fear of doing all wrong). I'm glad to see
The grass unmown; the scattering of daisies;
The hedges, overtopped by trees, unruly;
The cloud-filled sky, more bright than anything;
Our son's enquiring, quizzical expression;
My wife at 29, though plaintive, smiling.

COMMUTE

And if I were to lie
With my head in the grass,
Would there be tension still?

Yes, in the opposition
Between the sky, the grass;
The air, my body's impress.

My head's raging infant
Might be soothed by the grass,
Might be soothed by the sky

Or see only floaters there,
Tear fistfuls of the grass.
It would be something, though,

To park near the motorway,
Wade through the long grass,
Lie in it, facing the sky.

THE PASSAGEWAY

The junk-cluttered passageway is cleared.
What seemed like grime reveals itself as mould.
Maybe the air's enough to cleanse the space.
No, something's wrong. The new should not smell old.

This labourer has a wicked uncle look;
Good that he's working only on the outside.
The mould is hardly menacing, but still:
It's better to be rid of than to hide.

I picture large, translucent lozenges
(A different kind of mould, perhaps), like soap,
But cultivated from some helpful germ
To absorb the rot: a fantasy of hope.

There are germs in my dad's old army kit-bag.
They say kids aren't exposed enough to such.
I was exposed. This passageway's exposed.
At least mould's natural, soft to the touch.

IN THE GARDENS

The tomcat matched my stride along the hedge.
Was I, unwittingly, now putting others
In danger's path – this litter
Cooryying into Mama? No, it seemed
All lived convivially in the gardens.

As much as these railings, my fears when young
Cast a shadow. And the cat's got my tongue.

UNSCRIPTED

Living in this unscripted play,
You must resist the temptation
To over-act. The day-to-day
Has repetition, not revision.

You won't be needing Stanislavski
Where you are going on holiday.
And, anyway, how would you play
A breakdown, the death of a baby?

Studied intensity at one
With inarticulacy: soon
The kiss-me-quick hats will be on.
Make 'No high drama' your slogan.

SO MANY THINGS

On her 'Day of Big Remembering',
Your granddaughter left her doll in the car,
She had so many things to bring.

I wish you lived in memory
But it's no good, l can't remember
Though I left school and my hands are empty.

MISSING

'Crying won't find it – only looking can,'
I told my daughter, prompting her to rage:
'That's what happens when you're sad. That's
Absolutely a thing.' No gulf in age
Existed in that moment. I was back
At the windowsill, staring at a cage
Of boughs.
                My daughter, you are right to cry
And I am wrong to scold. My heart was torn
Once between stifled grieving, endless searching…

I'll help you find your plastic unicorn.

THE LANDLADY'S STORY

Our firstborn just born, on the second night
I stayed close by you (both) at a B&B,
Near-blind to the surroundings. The landlady
Answered my joy, not to congratulate.
'A woman devotes herself to her baby
So much she neglects her man.' And with that
She left me, key in hand, to forge a plot
Through every cheerless chapter of her story.

AWE

You the cathedral – vast, symphonic;
I the mouse, in a minor place.
What keeps me in awe? Something chronic.
I see organ pipes, not your face.

THE BED

1
We sat on the bed. 'I love you,' I said.
'What are you going to do about it?' she said.

2
Eyes strayed from the bed to the glowing curtain.
'Don't breathe a word of this to anyone.'

3
My breathless words have kept faith with the sun.

ME TO BE

You want to know what it's like here,
Then lie half-propped-up on your bed at dusk
And watch the branches sway in orange streetlight
Through a net curtain ideally.
At how many removes do you suppose
Me to be? As many as despair
From desperation. (Not desperate enough?
Picture a school assembly hall
With the public man telling the young to *strive*).
You want it set out in a note:
'I killed myself to keep my self alive'
Or some such. No, the branches sway
Without melodrama, unnervingly.

Here it's like nothing, like nowhere.

NOTE

I wish you hadn't had to write that note
To the postman. Your last considerate act
Was to prepare the finders of your body.
I hardly knew you, except in the way
We know anyone:
Immediately and absolutely.
You sat there with a tolerant, fixed grin,
Your wife probing me on my prospects (none),
And saw you wouldn't lose your daughter yet.
I peeled spuds from your crop (I could do that),
Helped set your stubble fields alight –
If running aimlessly, joyfully alive
Helped at all.

The wind can carry fire.
What were the circumstances
That fanned your hurt?
I wish you hadn't had to sit alone
In the farmhouse;
More, that I didn't have to write this note.

HOUSE WORDS

Car bien des années ont passé depuis Combray
– Marcel Proust

The words that made a terraced council house
A country home in Combray...

In pride of place, the mantelpiece:
Not Siena marble, its wealth
The coins of emptied pockets.
The gas fire never warmed it
As live coals did in Dad's day;
At least it was there to lean on.

The banister
A prop for jumping,
Too close to the wall to slide down
(We slid down it anyway);
The sofa, the chest of drawers, the cutlery...
It was all there, as in great houses,
However cramped it was,
However cramped we were.

So many spaces where our minds could lurk!
So many words for cupboards:
The one under the stairs,
The shoe, the sliding-door, the immersion
That warmed Mum's tights and the insurance money –
What Proust could have made of that!

We check ourselves
In different mirrors now,
For many years have passed since Blackbraes.

The words hold tight the memories.

DISCOURSE ON THE DIRT

SHE: I'm sick of all the talk
Of children's education
And, worse, career options.
I liked playing in the dirt.
Isn't that how life should start?

HE: I heard it in a dream:
The child knows everything,
Its just-born mind a pool
Unsullied by the dirt
Of all the knowledge we impart.

OLYMPIAN

for Dearbhla Rooney

There's force so natural nature can't resist,
Whether in glacial valleys or a boxer
Like this Olympian, Mullies' daughter, Dearbhla.
Her spirit: kindness that can form a fist.

LOOK, IT'S SNOWING

Say what you like about life
(And many have, and some still do),
It isn't meaningless.

How do I know this?

Once, in my teens, I argued with a friend.
Could there ever be such a thing
As a meaningless act?
I told him, no: nothing lacked meaning.
'Nothing?'
'Nothing.'
'Not even this stick?'

In my twenties, I was reminded of this
By Chekhov's Baron Tuzenbach –
That line to earnest Masha:
'Look, it's snowing: what does that mean?'

I shifted in my seat.
The Baron's words brought back
My father's death on New Year's Day,
The window-sill below my chin,
The branches of the window-tree,
Snow falling:
Beauty even in death,
And numbness.

So much for snow.
Don't get me started on sticks.

It's hardly the monk in his cell, is it?
Association isn't meaning, after all.

Tell that to the birds
In the winter tree,
The snow falling, pure
As the driven poem.

We must live.

INSULT

There's relish in observation.
'You're a black and white sort of guy,'
He scoffed. No call for any weapon:
There's devil's blood on the tongue of a magpie.

GIVING UP

My mum defied advice and stayed a smoker.
'It's the only comfort I have,' she'd say
So routinely I gave up my dismay
That I was no comfort to her.

THE DREAM'S END

I used to dream a knife-man stalked me
Through all the house to the dark room
I cowered in. He meant me harm
I could prevent by waking only –
So ensuring the dream's recurrence,
The fright I've never fully shaken since.

Last night I ventured up those stairs
In dream, clutching a kitchen knife,
And saw a bird afraid for its life
Nestling in its mother's feathers…
Don't be so angry with me, Mum:
It's good that I carried us out to freedom.

SERIOUS

In my grief
I watched the birds in the window-tree
But was not thereafter
A bird-watcher.

In adulthood
I drank God knows-what with God-knows-who
But did not become, when wiser,
A connoisseur.

Did I lack focus?
Well, yes, but I was also, always,
Rolling with the punches.
I'm serious.

NEXT DAY

I put my nose to the glass
To breathe in last night's whisky.

What do I feel – nostalgia
For even yesterday?

Yes, but mixed with regret
For all we couldn't say.

YOUR LIE

Not only
do I
deny
your lie
I
defy
any
one I
loved to try
to lie
so brazenly
to lie
so convincingly

AT 40

Does anybody any longer say,
Even ironically,
That life begins at 40?
To one who died on New Year's Day
In his 39th year sadly
None may.
But it's good, Dad, in a way
That you escaped the Hallmark jollity,
The quietly desperate complacency,
The turning grey,
And lived to prove that saying's true corollary
Its contrary,
'Life ends before 40';
In a way.

HOW TO SPEAK

I was lost for a word
Till my son showed me how to speak.
He said: 'I saw a bird
Carry a stick in its beak.'

EUPHORIA

1
Pity the driver
Who, eyes fixed on the middle distance,
Is jolted out of his mild trance
And overtaken by euphoria.

2
This church, the perfect symbol of my childhood,
Mixes Catholicism
With brutalism.
Up against brick walls, I tried to be good.

3
Why is it always so unreal
In the middle?
What began well soon turns to hell
Till once again we're normal people.

4
The mission priest comes in
To galvanise the congregation.
Such overdue elation
Warrants a less humdrum sin.

5
'Hello. How are you?'
'I'm alive,' I say.
It's something I say.
And you? Are you alive too?

6
The kids are mangling a hymn in the back.
'Circle of teeth, strong and false,' they sing.
'I've changed my mind – confession is great craic,'
You say. I am beside you, smiling.

THE LONGEST DISTANCE

Our ears prick up:
Tennessee Williams on the radio,
Voice filled with character ('and booze,' I sneer),
Relays his loneliness from forty years ago.
Once upon a time, in bed together,
We read his play *The Glass Menagerie*,
Laughed, touched
By fragile Laura Wingfield's
Pleurosis being mistaken for 'blue roses'.
Only the closing speech –
'Time is the longest distance between two places' –
Seemed off, like it couldn't apply to us.

'I DIDN'T DO WRONG, DID I?'

Elegant Parisian,
Always so welcoming, why now
Do you stand at your broad table
Unsmiling, perhaps unable
To entertain the thought of me?
Friendship's a cathedral
Which, if we damage, we restore
– Or is the damage, dear,
Irreparable?
Oh let me see you again
In your narrow kitchen,
Smiling, saying, 'Nothing
Has been done wrong.'

CONFESSION

'Hell, it's been a very long time.'
- *Rod Stewart and Martin Quittenton, You Wear It Well*

Is it forbidden to confess
I liked the offence to my intellect
Whenever she passed a church and blessed herself
Or said 'dear love her' as a mark of respect?

I noted Keats comparisons
And contrasts in the words of songs I knew,
But danced with her to Rod's 'You wear it well,
Madame Onassis got nothing on you.'

And when I parsed a Love Heart's syntax
Light-heartedly, she took the pen from me,
Wrote: 'Did you invent Loathe Hearts?' I confess
I liked being shamed by that profundity.

THE LOVES

The Loves' farm was a stone's throw from my aunt's.
It was the Loves' milk, udder-warm, that tipped
Out of the metal churn to my aunt's table;
Their hayloft we climbed into and jumped from
(The Loves' eyes burning or else turned aside).
The name would fill the air, like the third chapter
Of St Paul's first letter to the Corinthians:
We were always hearing 'Loves this', 'Loves that'.
No, I shouldn't have shied away from them,
For though 'the Loves' still resonates, I can't
Recall the Loves themselves, their talk, their faces.

MOTHER MARY

My mother was called Mary,
Occasionally May,
But never Molly.
Me, I was Christ to her Mary,
May-not to her May,
And might have been jolly
If she'd ever been Molly.

CIVILITY

When I see the bloated autocrat
Bring his tiny fist down on the screen
And fear civility's at an end,
I ponder a park's giant chess-set;
My aunt's tiered cake-stand; long unseen,
The delicate mother of a friend.

WICHITA LINEMAN

There is perfection in the imperfection of the rhyme
That keeps the Wichita lineman jarringly on the line.

OR WHAT?

What have I read in my life,
Or what have I seen,
That I find myself writing,
Even in fun,
To someone who cares:
'I only care a little; still,
Every little hinders'?

ISOBEL GOWDIE

It starts with a drone, on and on,
This requiem for a witch, for a woman
Who could fly like straw when she wanted –
Or so she said, and so they noted down.
Poor Isobel Gowdie, mad Isobel Gowdie,
A truant from the School for Wives:
Were weaving and weeding not enough for you?

You danced in the hills, with the night sky souls
Rising or falling
To a disturbance of drums,
Then told it all
In presence of the Notary Public –
Every conceivable inconceivable horror
And the size of the devil's member.

A gat in in the shape o a jaikdaw…
Nou a hae nae pouer at aw.
We hate what we lack:
In these men, Woman.
Poor, mad Isobel Gowdie,
Whatever wrong you'd done,
Gone into a hare, you outran them all.

AT DUSK

I left you back there, back then. While my world
Grew colourful, my work a lovely war,
You sat at dusk and filled in applications.
Then doubts. Who did I love? What was I fighting for?
By Christmas, all was over. Once or twice
We met up to make sure, as lovers will.

I'm dreaming of Surrey because I'm sorry.

Think of me when you have an hour to kill.

YOU HAVE TO GO

A digger churns up next door's earth.
The crows are wheeling overhead.
We try to talk, for what it's worth,
Above their din. But nothing's said.

For reasons that you don't restate
There is no hope, you have to go.
I will be – what? Not dead, not yet,
And not the man you used to know.

NOSTALGIA REVISITED

Cat owners used to second best
Whose preferences were unexpressed;
Kids who never felt quite full,
Unglowing on the trek to school;
Girls whose eyes would scour bookshelves,
Not dote on dolls that wet themselves;
Women who weren't content to sing
And dance while doing the vacuuming...
The glamour of that lost decade
Covers up the faded, frayed,
Or else just differently prized:
Our lives were not as advertised.
Think, while the New World Symphony
Plays over homespun poverty:
This was the liveliness of youth
You must now substitute with truth.

A SECOND TIME

I'd live my life a second time
Submerged, like a water spider,
And have your sun-reflecting eyes
To aim for. There'd be no forgetting
This time. And so the weeds would wave
And part, scene after scene unfolding.
The same fervour, the same sting
Would still be there: the joy of seeing,
The pain of losing, you again.
But first there is the joy, with you
Dismounting at the door while I
Run (though underwater) through
Room after room to greet you. Let
The end return to the beginning
And *how it is* be *how it was* –
This time there will be no forgetting.

THE WINTER OF BOB DYLAN

'Britons really were happier in the "good old days", according to a new study... Spirits sank during both world wars, but researchers at the University of Warwick found the lowest point was during the Winter of Discontent in 1978.'
– The Independent

The talking heads talked dolefully with glee
While uncollected bins, unburied dead
Were strewn across the screen. Gloom featured heavily,
Leading the Evening News with Kenneth Kendall,
Then News at Ten with Reginald Bosanquet
(Too true that spirits sank). Indefinite –
Or was it infinite? – strikes were the order
Of the day. This was my day. These were all
My salad days, some of them impaired
By old-new trauma unrelated to
Government pay caps. Like Beckett's Krapp,
I wouldn't have them back is what I'd say.
And yet the nation's lowest point was not
My own. 78: the year Bob Dylan,
Sounding a little crazy, a lot jaded,
Broke my delicate young mind like a vase
Then reassembled it, by sleight of hand
Somehow increasing its worth.
So, no.
Whatever research says, there were worse days.
That discontented season warrants praise.

BILLY FULLERTON

In response to Edwin Morgan's 'King Billy'

Razor gang founder, Mosley Blackshirt,
He's where he should be – in the dirt.
Let the guiltily cerebral
Feast on this waster's funeral:
I won't sell myself for a song.
And, yes, it will be – for as long
As we lend credence to such stuff –
Grey over Riddrie right enough.

PROG ROCK

Excess's promise is – it will be endless,
But why the jets were seized, capes cast aside,
Had less to do with taste than snaking dole queues.
When punk said No, we crowed. That music died.

FLIBBERTIGIBBET

The further it got from death,
The more of a flibbertigibbet
My mind became.

Tied to my living breath,
It dipped and rose like a kite
Unused to freedom.

There was some ballast with death:
I was told as a kid (so absurd)
I worked like a Trojan.

The death was my father's death.
Now my mind is a heavy bird
As I near my own.

GOD THE FATHER

It hasn't been easy, addressing God
As Father when my own father died early
(Early for him, early for me) and so
Acquired, in my eyes, near-divinity:
I never saw him faltering or frail.
No men who hung around could substitute
For his lost warmth their cold authority.
I saw some try, but I was too astute.

A worshipper, I knew my case was flawed.
For all my talk, what did I have to show?
A self-developed photo, a greased hand-tool?
My time in the wilderness made me odd,
But I recovered well enough to know
Men can be loved, and God is fallible.

THE RAIN

Nothing falls like the rain
Lulling you to sleep again;
The fall of resignation,
Of soothed or endured pain.

Whatever, or however, your pain,
It's good that you can sleep again.
There's no need to explain.
Nothing falls like the rain.

IN THE OFFICE

She doesn't turn her head before she speaks.
'Nobody climbs the stairs the way you do.'
I've tried to vary how I do for weeks.
The stealth's in me, whatever it is due to.

ADMISSION

'Remember to make your mind be elsewhere.'
I've never needed that advice, my dear.
Elsewhere's my usual place of residence:
I got in young and haven't moved out since.
Now the procedure's over, more than ever
I need to be with you here, only here.

THE ONE POSSIBLE

I've gone through life not really listening
To the one possible voice that could sustain me.

I heard it in a cave, the tent my knees made,
Bolstering me while nearby night mares sniffed the air.

Was Samson only lied to by Delilah,
Zhivago's love for Lara mere adultery?

I'm out in the open, love, battered as ever,
In need of you on this subsiding pier.

MY BEARING

I stood like a little Hitler,
Thwarted, angry and (God knows) sad
On the holiday promenade.
The crew-neck jumper I remember,

The crease of a frown I still have.
Maybe I'd failed to win a goldfish
Or lost at crazy golf. I wish
My bearing had embodied love.

But loss of a different sort
Lay underneath. It left a mark
So deep I'm mired in the dark
Still, doing and undoing hurt.

MISS QUIGG

Miss Quigg is dead, and will not beg our pardon.
Her *just-so* in an age when anything goes
Distinguished her – as if, in a fecund garden,
There grew, alone, a thin-stemmed issueless rose.

Once she presented me with a bone china
Commemorative mug whose wedding bells
Swung atop a smiling Charles and Diana.
I loved it, though I said I loathed all royals.

Her other gift, a book on Italian art,
Somehow managed to have no nudes in it,
But I had need of nudes. We grew apart.
I thought of her less as woman than as spirit…

Miss Quigg, you couldn't make up for my loss.
But Jude, your favourite saint, is my son's name.
And so too late I sense your case and cause
Were something like my own, if not the same.

BACK IN TIME

I'm not here to interrogate,
Uncover truth but act too late,
Or even lay a soothing hand,
Warbling that I understand.
I'm not interested in who lied;
I came here only to provide
A moment's company to one
Squinting like Popeye in the sun.

GOLD OR GLORY

Me once: slumped in a deckchair out the back,
Reading a wholesome Reader's Digest book
Which told the story of Heinrich Schliemann
Gazing upon the face of Agamemnon –
Only, he hadn't; his discovery
Went further back than that.
                                                My own history
Had its funeral mask – hardly gold, rather
The skin over the cheekbones of my father,
Not that his death was openly acknowledged:
Even a truth that's glaring can be dodged.
My dig for it, careful and conscientious
(Unlike old Heinrich's) unearthed only dross.

A snooze in the sun, by dint of alchemy,
Has made it shine, at least. A moment's glory.

SHERLOCK HOLMES

I let loose the bloodhounds
That hungered for adventure.
At the end of the school day
They'd doze a while, then stir.

I read through every case:
The Blanched Soldier, the Lion's Mane,
The Solitary Cyclist,
The Empty House, the Second Stain…

Mr Ferri twitched his gown
And the tales lost their force.
'Great fun,' he said, on reading one;
'Worthless as literature, of course.'

WHISKY

They say
A dash of water in a dram will bring
Out the flavour more.

What do I care what they say?
When did I ever dilute anything
In my life before?

ALL THOSE OTHER DAYS

Don't dwell on why
That day the suicide
Chose to die.

Wonder at
His choosing to live on all those other days;
Wonder at that.

NEXT TIME

'I've never been on a beach where there's snow.
I'd like to see that.'
                                        I will take you there
Next time they forecast snow – not pack the car;
Whisk you off so whim-like you won't say no.
I couldn't blindfold you, but you'll be blind
To my intentions, disorientated
In your own townlands, where you'll know the road
Better than I, but mutter: 'I don't mind.'
And when the tufts of marram grass stick up
You'll still not guess, or guess but still not say,
And I will lead you, hand in hand, the way
I used to do, when nothing was made up,
Then leave you to yourself, to walk the beach
Which I'll not sully, though I've sullied much.

WAYS

Your happiness holding your baby
Or shaping hot glass from the furnace
Shone in your face.

You'd ask me to check your copy,
Still grateful for advice I'd given:
To say what you mean.

I have been too slow to embrace
And the moments I choose to do
Can irk you.

'Affection isn't that or this.'
Best you peel spuds without my touch:
I've learned this much.

I love you – yes, in my own way.
I wish I loved you in your way.
But I mean what I say.

THE RUSE

In estate-agent-speak, they were luxury apartments;
The inhabitants of one, a gilded Steptoe and Son.
Under the nose of the stairwell's video intercom,
I fanned out a deck of cards, face down, then flipped it over –
To the old man's cackling amusement, not expertly done.
This ruse to nip in undetected ahead of the son
Worked wonderfully. Watcher, eavesdropper, interloper,
I was on the inside looking out. I was in danger:
One stray word from the father, and the son's ears would prick up.
If I couldn't catch all, I could catch and decipher hints.
What was a good hiding place? Unpromising the bare room,
And the bare room behind it, and the bare room behind that.
But in the last of all, an open window, a short drop
To the fatherless, sonless ground with its breathable air.
I wobbled then: remain as witness, or leave like a cat?

Might as well take a leap, see if the truth can put down roots.
I have heard enough in my life from crooks and substitutes.

FROM SOLITUDE

A mother to her daughter
Gazing out over the water:
'Back up you come, honey.'

I would not be without
The love that puts paid to doubt
For lust nor money.

My sense of you is thorough
As church bells rouse Hillsborough
And the children play –

Like the sudden certitude
That saved us from solitude
It seems only yesterday.

LOVE ON THE COSTA BRAVA

Cuando sale la luna
se pierden las campanas
– Lorca

The fake flamenco boys were out in force
Along the caves to trap the English girls.
I drank it all in, drunk. My head was turned
By talk of strummed guitars and gypsy blood.
We snared a couple of the girls ourselves
Until I blew it, stripped beside the waves,
My boyish body on the moonlit sand
Leaving the interchange between us... strained.

When the moon comes out the bells fade away –
The poetry outshines the fakery.

BRIDGES REVISITED

When I was in my teens, I wrote
'Bridges have always fascinated me' –
Innocent enough stuff, surely –
Then grabbed the reader by the throat.

The bridge I had in mind led to a grave
Where I would pray as I was told
For one whom only time travel could save.
Death was, invariably, my chokehold.

I smuggled darkness in the daylight,
The occult nestled in the bridge's mesh;
Enlisted beauty for the fight,
Ditched it before it ripened into fetish.

The throat, though, was my own, perhaps one teacher's.
Even now, I can't cross a bridge
Without a scent of garage flowers,
A vibration, setting my teeth on edge.

IN THE EPILEPTIC COLONY

1

'Ye shall know them by their husks: the wheat and the barley.'
On days off, we tramped through fields, through time
In watery sunlight
Towards the station, the platform spick and span,
Its hanging baskets
The censers of our altered days.

Here they come,
Almost an army of them, from
Liverpool, Belfast, Sunderland, Glasgow –
Wherever, in the UK, labour's cheap –
Sufficient hands to tend
A bumper crop of children in the fields.
Gather ye care staff while ye may:
Orion's Belt's above,
Stockbroker belt's below;
And set apart,
Nearer the racecourse than the gallows,
The staff hostel, a hive of cells,
'Colony' still stitched into the rough blankets.
Whispered instructions; kissed cheeks, lips; wiped eyes –
The warden tolerates the last goodbyes.

In Dormansland,
England leads a merry dance.
Armchair detectives but no crime.
Tarantula in aspic on the bar.
A harvest moon, a falling star.
Take it all in, in a single glance.
'We are leaving Downing Street for the last time.'

What a piece of work is a child
Whose cerebral neurons clack together
Much too erratically for normal life.
This one might have been born that way;
This one fell ill on holiday;
This one fell from a tree.
The case files tell you all their stories.
And still some older folk
Shy away from collection cans:
The falling sickness conjures devils for them.
Try not to sentimentalise these children,
Opining they are 'human, all too human',
Though by their smiling they would seem to say so.

Get them up.
Walk them into the bowl room.
See that they put on their uniforms
(Laid out by the night shift).
Serve them breakfast from the trolley.
Have breakfast yourself from the trolley.
Put toothpaste on their toothbrushes.

Walk them back into the bowl room.
See that they brush their teeth.
Give them their morning medication.
Make up the evening medication.
Walk them to school.
Go back and clean the House
(The blue paste's for the bowl room).
Make tea, if you like, and chat
But use this time to write
Incident Reports, record seizures.

And if, instead of 'Get them up,'
You hear 'Get the mop';
If in the bowl room you start to sing
'Danny Boy', only for one
To ask 'What are the pipes calling?';
If you see, in the only room still lit,
The outline of the doctor
Who presides over all, and who looks
Like some Socratic goat
(And whose wife, left alone,
Walks the grounds with an actual goat);
If you stare at the medication tray
Unsure if it's the morning's or the evening's;
If you spend one day in the Colony,
It will be this day, over and over.

2

Here's the door –
Green, as in the song – to the netherworld.
The warden, Lucy, with her sausage dog
Sees without looking up, don't ask her how.
If you're a woman, you turn to the left;
If you're a man, you turn to the right (though
Teens, twenty-somethings will turn where they please) …
'You have a bank of phones, a TV room,
A snooker room, and various small kitchens
For snacks only (meals in the dining hall).
The grounds are yours to walk in. There's no curfew.
(Be careful if you can't be good. One girl
Fell pregnant last term – obviously, she's
No longer in our employ.) Lock your door.
Smoking's permitted. Clean the bath after you
And good luck.'

Twelfth of July, and half the Belfast lot
Barbecue for King Billy
(A Glaswegian with jaunty hat joins in,
Says 'Get your party head on,'
And 'Do you want ketchup or brown sauce with that?')
You've heard them in the TV room discussing
Needlessly opening bags for inspection
In London stores; good chat-up lines to charm
Squaddies at checkpoints.

They sit and tut at silhouetted figures
On *Panorama*;
Reminisce, on both sides: soda farls,
Brown lemonade, and even UTV's
Continuity man.
Arguably, they are the foulest-mouthed,
Which is saying something.

If the answer is no,
You'll wander, a lost soul, past honeyed cells,
Detect a cruel edge to sudden laughter.
You'll stop to speak uncynically
And see a face light up, but it will be
The wrong face. You'll scan the doors, time your cough
For her precious door, its precious number,
Then crawl back to your room
With 'Richard, why don't you open that door?'
Playing on your radio-cassette. And still
The fate of it will need drilled in your brainpan,
So a note will be slipped under your door,
Handwritten, not by her.
                                        One day she'll knock
Figuratively, you near past all feeling,
Three times on the ceiling.

Set apart in 60 acres,
Near Tudor Lullenden, once Churchill's home,
And near East Grinstead –
Home to the poet-Supertramp, Davies,
Where Edward Thomas first met Robert Frost:
The one-time Epileptic Colony
In Lingfield, where the racecourse is.

And though one broke down after seeing a ghost
(The ambulancemen spirited her away);
And though another got her just deserts
On the back of years of minor cruelty
(Seen later with a pram, a face like fizz);
And though that Machiavellian, ex-army –
I have not seen a dapper Jack so brisk –
Fell short when he achieved authority;
There is just the one face that floats upstream
Demanding recognition. So, allow
Him that. He's here, unfresh from drinking solo,
Not as on summer evenings in The Plough
When the craic was good. Well, he's not gone back
On his word. Regard him, his bony brow
In troubled contemplation on a bridge,
No jaunty hat on now.

3

In the fields of sleep,
The Harvest King has come
With ears of wheat and barley in his hands.
Feet in the crumbling dirt
Of this muck-slope, slide down and see
The swarms of children hanging in the fields
From scarecrow posts, soaking up the sun;
In the evening, they are let down
To gather round the bonfires, chanting,
Chattering and chanting
The likes of

What is your favourite crow,
Hooded or carrion, raven or rook?
Who comes again tomorrow
Will get a second look.

The mothers wipe the brows, in classic fashion,
Of the hurt young. *Human, all too human,*
You think to mouth, but ponder at the flies
That live in time like you with no disguise.
The unmoving hands of the station clocks,
The rotted timetable saying East Grin, Ox,
Seem like a world away. Green branches hiss
On the flames; green branches above white branches.
One girl gets up, the music starts to play
Cheerlessly a *Come-Death* roundelay
While parched lips open to the proffered cups.
Repeated cries are heard, the music stops;

Reddening the edges of the nothing new,
Grotesquely birdlike clouds soar into view.

'How was your shift?'
'Bit weird. There's a full moon tonight.'
'You don't believe in that.'
'I don't know.'

The tents are pegged,
The yellow ducks all lined up in a row,
The bunting ends tucked into the marquee.
The iced cakes look resplendent in their dishes.
While raffle tickets flutter in the breeze,
The dedicated teacher taps
The cricket stumps into the new-mown grass.
Shoes have been shined for Lord and Lady Muck,
Hair parted with a watered comb,
And out they troop, like spoilers of the scene,
Pleased as Punch on this July morning
In Surrey, England.
Add to the mix a bloke from *On the Buses*
And, finally, the guest of honour,
Sporting a look of permanent surprise,
A straw-haired man who grins from ear to ear.

'Mother, this is your son ...'

In the waking fields,
Kids are deposited, their cases
Put into storage, toothbrushes
Dropped into the numbered cups.
This first day ambles on, administratively,
Till medicated heads begin to nod
And it is bowltime.
The duvets in the dorms are smooth as snow.
Tomorrow the autistic boys will start
To build Balloonland, with balloons and sticks,
And water it as if to make it grow
(The gardener will dump it in his trailer later).
And so they'll stay,
Be driven here and there in Sunshine coaches,
At the mercy of the merciful or merciless,
But always at the mercy of.

In the evening, chanting
Chattering and chanting

Try out my old black coat,
Wear my hat at a glance.
Prefer the fur of the English stoat.
On your knees, dance.

IN A DARKER VEIN

IN A DARKER VEIN

Cycle for piano and recitation, set by David Jaeger, 2020

IN MEMORY OF

'You'll not remember him,' they say,
As if pleased by the certainty.
Can't they see
It's you who'll not remember me?

WHITENED

The sky had set its face against
Competing drifts of snow, and lost:
Skirting the whitened, wooden-fenced
Green spaces that lay pure, uncrossed,

I leant into the wind, my hood
Left down because I was in awe
And done with being a child for good,
And clenched my fist and clenched my jaw;

Still, not left wholly in the lurch,
My alcove-loving, haunted mind
Entered the brutalist brick church,
Counting on darkness to be kind.

THE FALL

'You'll have further to fall,' she said,
'If the life you have constructed
Doesn't fit who you are.' I said:

'Like Alice down the rabbit-hole,'
As if to glamorise the fall
And dodge the hardness of it all

– Although if distance has much sway
In how I'll land or who I'll be
I don't know, and she didn't say.

NO REFRAIN

HE: In a darker vein
My blood will rise to mangle and to crush
Your hopes of getting underneath my skin
Then let you in, to listen
While it conducts a symphony of pain
This blood will horrify
Topple you in a head-rush
Lie in wait when you think it on the wane
It will pacify
With one eye on the spoils, then flare again
In a still darker vein
There's no refrain

SHE: At least yours is a *symphony* of pain
I've heard discordant noise
From bigger boys
Who ran away, as they are wont to do
Thanks, but I let myself in
While you busied yourself with meat I'd thrown
You think my blood can't rise or flare
In a darker vein?
Look, you've always known
I'm there with you
The refrain is, there's no refrain
I can do menace with a straight face too

THE ALARM BELL

From under green netting
That seemed filched from a cage,
He looked at me so steadily;
In appearance, a junkie or dead sailor.
Itinerant, almost feral,
He and his whole family
Were bristling in the car like cornered cats.
'Where have you been hiding, then?'
I asked, fake-nonchalantly,
All the time his eyes held me
Dying to get away.

The next day woke to rage
That coloured the day greenly
And I saw him there
And knew he was myself,
The cornered family my family.
That's when he rang the alarm bell,
Yelled: 'You're back on the junk.
You've drowned in the sea again.'

THE HOUSE AND YOU

The house and you were beautiful.
The scene was set so perfectly
For my repentance:
You took me in your arms.
The vista of forgiveness
Narrowed further.
You learned from my distress
You had no time for weakness.

Except the you was not the real you,
The me not quite myself.
And the house?
A leak had flooded
The foundations. Our neighbour said,
'The beauty of it is
The leak's a spring.
Get that hooked up, and you'll be laughing.'

THE RED DEER

The red deer took one look and sized me up.
I played for time – backed off, kept my head low.
Wind through the whins the narrowness of fate.
Time can't be played for on the moors.
The fate the red deer left me's not to know –
Was she the truth, the arrow, or the gate?

A BLESSING

I call a blessing
Down on your head.
A shadow's moving
In the oyster bed.

I hear a whisper
In the loudest room.
I see an angel
Perched on my tomb.

Angel oh angel,
Put down your pen.
Did I love enough?
Will I see her again?

GIFTS

Child of the light, I bring you
Fresh handfuls of wild flowers
From fields you do not visit.
I bring them. Don't despise them,
Though you find their scent bitter.

They can be arranged, so,
Into a wreath of heartbreak.
But it will wither.
The fields will be drenched again
By the sweet waters.